A Light Song of ̄

KEI MILLER was bor ̄ .... ̄era
Rubin Fellow at Yaddc ...., at the
University of Iowa, and .... ِnting at the
University of Glasgow. H .... ِe the short story
collection *The Fear of Stones* .... ِ06; shortlisted for the
Commonwealth Writers First .... ِze), and the novels *The Same Earth* (2008) and *The Last Warm. Woman* (2010), both published by Weidenfeld & Nicolson. His previous collections of poetry are *Kingdom of Empty Bellies* (Heaventree Press, 2006) and *There Is an Anger That Moves* (Carcanet, 2007). He edited the Carcanet anthology *New Caribbean Poetry* (2007).

Also by Kei Miller from Carcanet Press

There Is an Anger That Moves

as editor
New Caribbean Poetry: An Anthology

KEI MILLER

A Light Song of Light

CARCANET

First published in Great Britain in 2010 by
Carcanet Press Limited
Alliance House
Cross Street
Manchester M2 7AQ

A CIP catalogue record for this book is available from the British Library

ISBN 978 1 84777 103 2

The publisher acknowledges financial assistance from Arts Council England

Supported by
ARTS COUNCIL
ENGLAND

Typeset by XL Publishing Services, Tiverton
Printed and bound in England by SRP Ltd, Exeter

There is no night in Zion
There is no night there
Hallelujah, there is no night there
Jah Rastafari is I light
And we need no candlelight
Hallelujah there is no night there

Rastafarian hymn

Everybody must bring their own portion of Light
in this particular time

Lorna Goodison

Contents

Day Time

Night Time

Day Time

Twelve Notes for a Light Song of Light

i   A light song of light is not sung
        in the light; what would be the point?
        A light song of light swells up in dark
        times, in wolf time and knife time,
        in knuckle and blood times; it hums
        a small tune in daytime, but saves
        its full voice for the midnight.

ii   A light song of light spits from its mouth
        the things that occasionally gather:
        the dull taste of morning and cobwebs
        (you would not believe their thickness),
        and the strangest word – *caranapa* –
        so much larger than its letters, a Maroon
        of a word and a word so silent
        it is the opposite of song.

iii   A light song of light occasionally stutters.
          This is par for the course.
          There is no need for concern
          no need for bed-rest or vitamins
          no need to take your song in
          to the song specialist for treatment.

iv   But were you to take your light song in
          for a thorough checking-up, a blood screening,
          you might discover your song has cancer,
          HIV, diabetes, is going blind in its left eye.
          You may not have strength to sing
          your song for this season or the next.
          But a light song of light cannot be
          held back. It cannot wait on health
          or its perfect occasion.

v   A light song of light meditates in the morning,
        does yoga once a week, accepts the law
        of karma. It may not worship in a synagogue
        it may not worship in a balmyard
        but still it believes in a clean heart
        in righteous living and the general
        avoidance of pork. It would like to touch
        your feet, pronounce a blessing
        before you go:
            Jah guide and protect always.
            Selah.
            Ashe.
            Ashe.

vi   A light song of light will summon daffodils,
        bluebells and strawberries, humming birds;
        will summon silver, the shine of sequins,
        the gold of rings – and the dreadful luminosity
        of everything we had been told to close
        our eyes to (because they had no sharp
        edges, because they could not be wielded
        against our enemies) will be called back into service –
        retired weapons that have no memory of war,
        or that they could fight, or that they could win.

vii   A light song of light is not reggae,
        not calypso, not mento or zouk,
        not a common song from a common island,
        not a song whose trail you have followed for umpteen
                              years,
        a song trembled from the single tooth of
        the Singerman – the Singerman who had beat his tune
        out from a sheet of zinc
        and how it surprised you, the thin bellies
        from which music could be drawn.
        You did not know then that his song came
        at the price of history and cane
        and the terrible breadth of oceans: a price
        which, even now, you cannot fully consider.

viii   A light song of light don't talk
        the way I talk most days.
        To tell the truth I never know at first
        what this country was going do me –
        how I would start hearing myself
        through the ears of others,
        how I would start putting words on a scale
        and exchange the ones I think in
        for the ones I think you will understand,
        till it become natural, this slow careful way
        of talking, this talk like the walk of a man
        who find himself on a street he never born to,
        who trying hard to look like nothing
        not bothering him. And maybe nothing wrong
        with a false talk like that, but that
        is no way to sing.

ix   A light song of light is not understood completely
          not in the moment it is sung
          and maybe not for months after.
          But it sings with a faith common
          in those who never lost their accents
          who talk their talk knowing, *tssst*
          you may not catch everything but chu –
          you will catch enough.
          And if you don't catch nothing
          then something wrong with your ears –
          they been tuned to de wrong frequency.

x   A light song of light tells knock-knock jokes
          and tells them in order
          to illustrate the most heartbreaking points.
          It is not that the song
          does not know the weight of sadness;
          it is not that the song
          does not take things seriously;
          it is not that the song
          needs to write one hundred times on a chalkboard –
          I will be heavy,
          I will be heavy, I will be heavy, I will be heavy…

xi   A light song of light is distant cousin
        to songs we sing in bath tubs,
        is related then, by accident, to water
        and to soap and to square white tiles
        that bounce sound one from another,
        is related also to rain and to blankets
        and to the little things we say
        to get us through the hurricane.

xii   A light song of light says thank you
        to the paper it is written on –
        this most solid evidence of its existence
        however thin. Sometimes though,
        a light song of light wishes it were written
        on material even thinner, the shaft of morning
        that slides through a shut window.
        A light song of light believes nothing
        is so substantial as light, and
        that light is unstoppable,
        and that light is all.

This Zinc Roof

This rectangle of sea; this portion
Of ripple; this conductor of midday heat;
This that the cat steps delicately on;

This that the poor of the world look up to
On humid nights, as if it were a crumpled
Heaven they could be lifted into.

God's mansion is made of many-coloured zinc,
Like a balmyard I once went to, *Peace*
And Love written across its breadth.

This clanging of feet and boots,
Men running from Babylon whose guns
Are drawn against the small measure

Of their lives; this galvanized sheet; this
Corrugated iron. The road to hell is fenced
On each side with zinc –

Just see Dawn Scott's installation,
A Cultural Object, its circles of zinc
Like the flight path of johncrows.

The American penny is made from zinc,
Coated with copper, but still enough zinc
That a man who swallowed 425 coins died.

This that poisons us; this that holds
Its nails like a crucified Christ, but only
For a little while. It rises with the hurricane,

Sails in the wind, a flying guillotine.
This, a plate for our severed heads;
This that sprinkles rust

over our sleep like obeah;
This that covers us; this that chokes us;
This, the only roof we could afford.

Some Definitions for Song

for Richard and Natalie

— the speech of birds, as in birdsong, but with exceptions.
Pigeons do not sing. Vultures do not sing.   A bargain, or a
very small sum, as in 'he bought it for a song'. Think what we
could purchase with songs, thrown across the counter and
landing more softly than coins. Perhaps then, the origin of the
expression, to sing for your supper.   The troubled sound that
escapes from a woman's mouth while she dreams of fire, also
any sound that escapes, also anything that escapes; a passage
out, the fling up of hands. A prison break is a song. The parting
of the Red Sea was a song. In Israel there are many songs, but
there should have been six million more. Across the Atlantic,
there are many songs, but we needed ten million more.
Sòng (宋國) was a state during the Eastern Zhou Spring and
Autumn Period (770–476 BC). Its capital was Shangqiu.
Anything that climbs is a song; vines are a song; my father,
seventy years old, at the top of the ackee tree is a song; all
planes are songs. Song was a low-cost airline operated by Delta.
Tourists were flown by Song to Florida. Song's last flight was
on 30 April 2006.   All that pleases the heart. All that pleases
the ear. The final measure of joy. When we have lost song, we
have lost everything.   A common surname in Korea, often
transliterated as Soong. What would it mean if your name was
Song?   Song is the third and final album of Lullaby for the
Working Class. It was released 19 October 1999.   Songs
often refer to songs, as in 'He shall encompass me with a song';
'Sing unto the Lord a new song'; 'Sing a song of sixpence'.
Sing a song. Sing a song.

Until you too have journeyed

Until you too have journeyed through caves,
through miles of damp and bats, the cool
of all that is not living; until your one torch
has flickered out and you have found yourself
in a dark so dark you forget your eyes
or if they are opened; until you've had to find
a way, inch by careful inch, stopping to invent
an arrow out of wind; until you discover
how the feel and sound of stone or pebble
can exist without an image, the very thought
of colour competing for the air; until you too
have lost the day and the day has lost you
and it dawns on you, how foolish to have come
willingly to where the dead are put – until then
do not scoff at what has become our common
language for tomorrow and hope, this bright opening,
this end of dark, this light at the end of the tunnel.

Some Definitions for Light (I)

— *[etymology]* photo, root word for light, hence photology – the study of light. Photometer – the measurement of light. Photophilia, the love of light; the photophilic are drawn helpless, like sunflowers whose round faces travel across the day like the hand of a clock, like Agatha who insisted on dying even though she was well. Photomania, an obsession with light – in 1974 a man was found sweating in his small room, surrounded by a congregation of lamps, 137 bulbs burning, even during the day he was trying to create. Photophobia, the fear of light. Photophobics hide in shadows; their eyes hurt. The photophobic cannot read this; they are at risk of going blind. Blindness could be called photominimus or photomaximus. It is, at once, the absence and the great excess of light – the belly of a cave and its opening. Photogenic – concerning the basic helix strands of light, and also the ability to birth light. A photographer is one who writes about it; a photograph is writing composed of it – of brilliant, brilliant light. Look. Look closely – this is a photograph.

If this short poem stretches

If this short poem stretches beyond
its first line, then already, already,
it has failed, become something else,
something its author did not intend
for it to become, a misbehaving,
rambunctious, own-way thing,
its circuitous journey a secret known
only to itself, its tongue its own.
The author is destined, I am afraid,
to write poems that escape him.
This, for instance, was to be just one
line long, or even one long line,
dedicated to Mervyn Morris and his love
of brevity, but it has become something else
entirely. The poem sings its own song,
reaches its own end in its own time.

Notice to the Public, Please Observe

a found poem

I am available Tuesdays–Thursdays, 10 a.m.
Tickets will be issued and you will be dealt with
at that time. After that I am paralyzzz, blinddd
defff and dummm. If you have a hard luck story,
don't come. If I don't know you, don't come.
If my friend is the one who know you, don't come.
If you need to renew a missing passport
in a hurry, don't come. If you need to be
recommended to an embassy, don't come.
If you need a firearm licence, don't come.
If you need to bail someone and you don't bring
a Form 2 from the officer in charge, don't come.
If you are a soldier or police who feel him is as large
as the law and bigger than God, don't come.
If you have things to do that you should do
and you don't do them yet, don't come.
If you can read and understand this then
you won't waste your time and come.

Found on the gate of the residence of a Justice of the Peace,
Portmore, Jamaica. March 2009.

Some Definitions for Light (II)

— *[noun]* The lungs of butchered animals are called lights. I have
sometimes wondered if they pray – if, before the blade falls,
cows and sheep and ducks fill their lungs with the weight of
their dying, the nothingness to come, if their final sounds are
light calling out to light.

The Longest Song

John Cage's composition 'As Slow As Possible' began being played in St Burchardi's Church, Germany in 2001 and is scheduled to end in the year 2640.

The longest song begins like a comma, a rest
that lasts for eighteen months. Long enough
that when the first chord is heard, surprising

as an extinct bird come back to life, many
cannot stop their tears. And one man
has told his wife he plans to weep

until the music has reached its next rest.
I suspect were we to pilgrim towards this
hymn, were we to sit in the hard pews

and only listen, patient through its months
of silence, our lives would be held
like a story my father tells me is true:

a man with a noose round his neck is allowed
one final song. He stands on the stage
and with a voice rivalling Franco Corelli, begins

ten billion green bottles standing on the wall.
And though this man has never lost count
of his bottles, all have lost count

of the years that have passed since,
the world outside the world of the song.
A hundred years at least they have stood still:

a man, his executioner, and the small crowd
of witnesses, all held as we too could be held
in a single room, our lives echoing

beyond their natural years, stretched
between clef and final fall, crescendo
and diminuendo, of one incredible song.

A Short Biography of the Singerman

The Singerman, born in 1903, has lived
in Spaulding, in Lime Tree Grove,
in a village called Rim – wherever
there were no roads, wherever the hills
rose up like a flock of green
parrots, you would find him.
Singerman, paid half shilling a week,
dug trenches, filled the pits with mortar
and bits of broken stone.
But Singerman's most crucial job
was to lift up mentos, time *chichi-bud-o*
to the swing of a workman's hammer;
and no one knew if it was the hammer
or if it was the song
but no rock was so strong
to resist the fourth accented beat –
that *huh* – in the Singerman's song.

Brochure

Avoid the three-lane highways;
drive on the Singerman's roads.
Your journey, even when bumpy,
will be sweet, the ascents lifting you
as in a chorus, the sharp corners
turning you like a force of melody.
There is a back road that sings
its off-beat way up Stony Hill –
built of course by the Singerman;
and the slim road to Mount Pleasant –
also built by the Singerman;
and yes, it was the Singerman
who orchestrated the long road
to Portland, made it full of waterfalls
so that a man and his mule
traversing the miles could forget,
for a while, the solemnity of their loads.
Please, when you visit Jamaica, drive
on the Singerman's roads.

What Can Be Accommodated

The Singerman's road can accommodate Benzes
and bicycles, Hondas and handcarts, your own
two feet, and the slow, complaining traffic of goats.
Colour blind cows have even been known
to read signs by their octagonal shapes
and stop. All God's creatures are welcome.
So long as you are heading somewhere,
the Singerman's road will take you there.

The Singerman's Papa

The Singerman's Papa was a Singerman
   He was always a–singing, o–ho
The Singerman's Papa went to Panama
   He went a–sailing, o–ho

The Singerman's Papa lost his song
   He went a–searching, o–ho
Went searching the dust that filled his lungs
   It was lost inside him, o–ho

The Singerman's Papa died in Panama
   He died a–digging, o–ho
But his song died long before he did
   It is buried inside him, o–ho.

The Colour of the Singerman's Songs

If the Singerman had gone to America
he woulda sung the blues
he woulda sung the blues
with a voice like John the Baptist
with a tongue covered in sand
and his blues woulda been that kinda blues
that is fed on locust and honey,
blues like a cry that cometh
from the wilderness, blues
like the sound of warthogs alarmed at the sky.
And the Singerman woulda sung it
from his field in Arkansas, straight
to Harold Arlen's sitting room
and Arlen woulda gone to the keys
to write a song more sad than 'Blues
in the Night'. But the Singerman did not go
to America. He stayed right here;
so bless up to him and his song and all music
that is sad in its own colour;
bless up to the notes that fall like flakes
of rust; bless up to every song that makes
its own way out of dungle, a path straight through
ghettoes; bless up to the mento which becomes ska
which becomes rubadub which becomes legend;
bless up all the red–gold songs, the weary evening time songs,
songs given to us by the Singerman.

In Defence of Obeah

was not just cat bones,
parrot beaks, the teeth
of alligators some would pat
our pockets in search of;
was not just poison brewed with shells;
was not just a way towards hell;

was not just a lock-up
of shadows in bottles
knowing man will surely dead
if his most basic shape is no longer
cast on ground; was not
just a duppy gather-round;

was not just a sundown
of candles, the wicks only
so long as the life of Massa;
was not just the slow
backward recital of verses;
was not just belly knotting curses;

it was all of that, but also
it was an anti-drowning
and it was all of that, but also
it was an anti-breaking
and it was all of that, but also
it was a knowledge
and it was all of that
and all of that
and it was

Questions for Martin Carter

The Guyanese poet Martin Carter was under such constant surveillance
that some of his poems have only been preserved because of
pictures government spies took of his fence.

About the poems you never wrote on paper
but on sheets of galvanized zinc – I would like to know
if you simply trusted the unpredictable shape
of each large letter, the rise and fall like waves that rippled
through your lines. I want to know if composing poems
on such strange surfaces changed them, and what
they could believe in, and what they could say,
and if such poems were conscious
of their unlikely readers – the woman
who after your death came scavenging through the yard
looking for a sheet of zinc to build her own flimsy wall
and roof; do the poems at night prophesy
to her needs, or against the men who snapped
photographs of your fence, deconstructing
the words every which way, trying to find in it
a plot, or a message: MENE MENE TEKEL.
And if suspecting this would be their way
into the world, published and kept
as files by a nervous government,
did the poems even bother to clap their hands
or sing, or rhyme? Did they say their message
as plain as prose, that this was the dark time
when brown beetles crawl
when guns take aim at our dreams
when we each should be found walking about
and groaning between the wind?

Call this apocalyptic propaganda if you must

Call this apocalyptic propaganda if you must:
The World Ended in the Spring of 2006.
But how much you are willing to accept this story
depends on how far your mind can stretch,
if you believe, quite frankly, in parallel universes,
the one thousand lives we lived simultaneously
and which could only be glimpsed through magic
mirrors or déjà vu. Well, what we most feared
would happen has happened. America, Iraq, Korea;
the pressing of buttons; the detonation of bombs
from one pole to the next; the grand explosion
of people who didn't even follow newspapers
or give a damn, because we were in the middle
of simple things like eating spaghetti or sneezing.
But here is the fantastic point: the fact that you
are now reading these lines, means you belong
to the only world that did not go bang, a world in which
some uncelebrated hero snipped a green wire
before the clock drained itself to zero; it means
you were destined to survive; were more special
than your 999 alternate selves; that your prayer
was heard above theirs. And what this poem will now say
on behalf of your saved ass is, how fucking cool is that!

For Cornelius Eady

Here it is now, the moment
I carry your book to a café;
here is the woman who stares
at the cover
and asks if I am you.
I should be hurt;
in this moment I am twenty-five,
you are already fifty
but what I feel is wonderful.
In a future moment you should lie
and say you feel this way too
and that every day it is wonderful
to be a poet in this world.
I smile at the woman who sees me
in you; within the frame of my dreaded
hair, behind a forehead, broad
as a mother's back,
recognises a man who could write biographies
for jukeboxes. Cornelius,
there is coming a moment
when I too will be fifty, and I hope then
to still have your face,
to smile at women who pour
cups of coffee in Jamaica.
I want them to lift our face to theirs
and hear us singing from our covers
How you gonna do, love?
– and the harmony –
Wha' you a guh do?

Thinkin Home

thinkin of scent, thinkin of accent,
thinkin of bombays, de sound of de fruit
fallin outside a window; thinkin how de thud
of mangoes can rhyme with morning;
thinkin of Mavis Bank, de riverbed like an acre
of grey, de stones bleached into sadness, thinkin
of de way up de Blue Mountains
cleared by Nanny's cutlass, de walk as long as Sunday,
de air that grows thin,
de smell of number that grows thick,
thinkin how it easy to forget de magic of mangoes
when you find yourself here
and you no longer wake to the hard accent of fruit falling.

Some Definitions for Light (III)

— [*adjective*] A comedian once said when life gives you AIDS make lemonade. And just how funny you find that, how high the crest of your laugh or how deep the depth of your silence, can be calculated – something to do with long division and the measure of the horizon that stretches from right shoulder to left; what I mean to say is that light as adjective, as that which can be borne easily, is as various as our shoulders.   The young who sneak into theatres make loud and raucous light of everything; they laugh even when the hero is killed.   There is a reason why heavy things are made light – because if they weren't we would grow old too quickly; we would march home and measure knives against our wrists.

Night Time

The Lost Prophecy of Alexander Bedward

This word this word this word is less
than it once was. this word has begged for peas
one mile to the next, made a slow, slow way
across water and years. this prophecy has lost
its prophets. this this this word belonged
it belonged to Elijah once, it was caught
up once upon a time, lived in a cloud
for a while, spoke cloud, prophesied cloud,
we were once like clouds, listen,
listen closely to the stammered broken
word, imagine what it once was
when it was when it was as whole
as bread. the word, broken and disclouded
limped like youknowwho to this new world and ate
its own small ration of saltfish and yam.
this old, old word that fell from the sky
and broke, this word which by all accounts
should have keeled over like Sammy,
it was found in August Town by a fasting man,
he had been fasting, he had been making space
a large space in his belly to fit this dwindled word
and though the word was dwindled and the space
was large, it was more, it was more than
Father Forsythe's cart of mangoes,
it was more than the man had ever swallowed.
this word, this word is more than you
have ever pronounced. when the man
from August Town said it, when he said
you are like clouds, you belong to sky, when
he called forth every wing which was hiding then
in the cavern of our songs, when he pulled us up
from out the river, up from off of Babylon ground
and said fly   fly   fly   fly   fly   fly   fly   away
truly, there were those who heard, who saw
what they could be in this word, who traded
the ground their feet would no longer walk on
for white cloth. truly it was doves they saw

inside this word. and the doves were who
they would become. listen, listen, this word
did not mean to break mind or wing or spirit,
this word did not mean to bring hunger
or madness, but the word's brokenness
was its truth, its truth, its stuttering was
its eloquence. this word was always full
of white bones. this word was a eulogy:
it says we are less than we once were,
as much as we will ever be again; it says
this is the dark time; mother, the great stone
shall not move; it says a terrible broom
has swept our rooms, now this is a place for owls.
oriabattacacacasandai. oriabattacacacasandai.
listen to this word.

Abracadabra

Used as a charm to ward off illness, the word was usually written out
in the form of a triangle.
Entry from *The Oxford Dictionary of Word Histories*

(a)pronounce the word slowly
(ab)one letter at a time breathe in
(abr)let the spell expand your chest
(abra)let thunder gather behind your teeth
(abrac)you need nothing so silly as wand or hat
(abraca)trust only in the syllables and in your breath
(abracad)believe only in the growing alphabet of the word
(abracada)its pyramidal shape that makes you think of Cholula
(abracadab)what is to come will descend like a waterfall river healing
(abracadabr)splashing onto your mother's bed wetting her unmovable legs
(abracadabra)this magic stretches Alpha to Alpha Root to Root Amen to Amen

Unsung

There should be a song for the man who does not sing

himself – who has lifted a woman from her bed to a wheelchair

each morning, and from a wheelchair to her bed each night;

a song for the man recognised by all the pharmacists, because

each day he has joined a line, inched forward with a prescription

for his ailing wife; there should be a song for this man

who has not sung himself; he is father to an unmarried son

and will one day witness the end of his name; still he has refused

to pass down shame to his boy. There should be a song

for the man whose life has not been the stuff of ballads

but has lived each day in incredible and untrumpeted ways.

There should be a song for my father.

Prologue

Say – crick, then wait for crack...
Say – once upon a time, a long, long time...
Say – riddle mi dis and riddle me dat...
Say – mmmhm... Say – eh-eh... Say – but 'tap...
Say – draw long bench...
Say – well mi dear... Say – as to how I did hear...
Say – Sister Vie pass through today, mouth full of story,
I not repeating for de gossip, but that we can pray
for Miss Mattie... Say – to God be de glory!...
Say – it has been going about... Say all what you must say
cause you don't pay tax fi yu mout...
Say – suh me get it, suh me give it...
Say – if it don't go suh, it nearly go suh...
Say – hear with your ears, but let your heart
be a light, and let light guide you safe
pass all that hide in the night
Say – crick, then wait for crack...
Say – story time, is now story time...

De True Story of Rolling Calf

Two bwoy with nothing but de devil
inside dem, a cricket bat in their hands

knock out de young bull but not hard enough.
He wake up somewhere between de hacking

through his back leg; and then mooing a sound
that draw poor people from their beds, he escape

into de night. A farmer turn to him wife
and say, I hear like a cow asking de moon

'Why me, why me?' De wife nod to say
is that she hear as well. So days pass

and gangrene take over, make de bull's back leg
useless, make him walk a walk like him was dancing

dip and fall back. Then bitterness grow like a phantom
leg; him start to wait in bamboo patches

or under bridges, just to take revenge on anything
that look human. Listen – de true story of Rolling Calf

is not that beast evil, but that man evil,
and every buck him get – is him who cause it.

De True Story of Nathaniel Morgan

In de archives of de now defunct JBC – before they did run out of reels
and had to tape over thirteen years of Roy Forrester making bad
prediction of de weather, tape over Dennis Hall asking school pickney
hard question, then tape over all de news for sake of no longer
being new, just more de same storm and murder, but in an early year –
there was footage of a woman, a baby-mother to judge by de rise
of her belly. You must imagine her face, press up gainst de news
camera, her tears rolling in a space between lens and cheek.
And she was talking and hiccupping for a man whose body
four police boys had made into a riddle. And in this footage
she is telling de camera bout a power that was inside him, that draw
her cross a swamp plenty evenings, how she risk de deadly bite
of alligators just to be with him on nights when de breeze did sound
like death approaching. And she did know it and him did know it –
that this death would be awful. And she say that knowledge made him
almost righteous – made him close as she would ever get to Jesus.
De camera pans out and she is holding de hem of her own garment,
de same one she once lent her man that he could escape de rope
of Babylon. De real real story of Natty Morgan is de story of de best
of men – that he lived longer than he should have, and he
had been loved by a woman.

De True Story of Coolie Duppy

She come on a boat from de east, traipsing
behind a man who was pure beast, cane-cutter
who did most of him cutting at home,

beat de girl like she was nothing more than piece
of turn meat. De child take bruises like man
might take his wages, like she know

de lord God have his mercy, but would never
give any to she. They bury her under a bombay
mango tree, and pray that each June would find

a soft, sweet fruit fallen on her breast. But
death find her every way but soft and sweet.
Vengeance draw her straight out from under

de tree, back to de house, and all
what she did fraid to give when living
she don't ramp to give when dead. Coolie Duppy

throw down torment; every night she draw back
her fist and beat her man in such a way
him could not believe that fist was made of mist.

Coolie Duppy now turn patron saint and guardian
to any woman who walk into doors or fall down
steps once a week, who lie beside men

whose snores stink of rum; any woman
who can't fall asleep at night, her bruises
pulsing in the dark, need only speak de name

that was written at de root of de bombay tree.
Just say, *Asha Janaki, Asha Janaki, come
Coolie Duppy, avenge me.*

De True Story of deLaurence

All who say deLaurence was just a man
that publish hocus-pocus books
    is all who never have houses burnt to de ground
    is all who never dangle keys
from de miggle of a bible
chanting by saint peter by saint paul
and see the key haul itself out
    is all them that don't care fi know
de whole truth of things.

But we who see with more than eyes
who know de bird that preach from on top de coffin
and make altar call for Mr Brown
was none other than deLaurence
come in a johncrow form

is we who understand
de story of a man is sometimes more
than that man.

Don't tell we bout deLaurence who
did only publish books,
who did only live in Chicago;
him did live nearer to we than that.
De stink of his breath on our necks
is as true and as close as night.

A Praise Song for Sudden Lights

for Michael Moineau, almost mugged

…and that I would understand the impulse
    to shout motherfucker, as if the blade pressed
against your belly had pushed up and out your throat
    all the anger of exile, you describe to me fear

larger than the spilling of guts – of losing yet another
    country and a language you had just begun to dream in –
how you knew then that your wallet was more
    than credit cards or euros – it was your woman,

and the room in Berlin you refused to let go of. Praise
    then to salvation which did not come from heaven,
but from two stories above – one light turned on, and then
    several – a whole avenue beaming out in response

to your cry for help, illuminating the face of a would-be
    robber who dropped knife and fled. Praise a decision
so small – the flicking of a switch, that could give you back
    your life. And praise to the neighbours whose faces are still

unknown, but whom you imagine as squares of yellow –
    how magnificent, the suddenness of yellow that could
puncture the belly of evil, and night. O that we each,
    in our hours of greatest need, be rescued by light.

A Creed

When you no longer know God
when you are no longer sure
that you ever knew him;

when you are done praying
with your fingernails,
with your eyes pressed into the sand,
with your teeth broken against the pavement;

when you are done with speaking to the silence
wishing that the silence would hear;

when you are done with waiting
at galleries or in music halls,
waiting to gasp at the beauty
of things, waiting
to fall in love;

when you are done slamming doors
that were not relevant to anything,
done shaking houses, and making plates
jump from their shelves;

when you are done throwing bricks
into the seats of parked cars
shouting – this if for that boy
who was killed,
shouting – this is for the taxes
that were raised;

when you are done with the news
because it no longer breaks your heart,
and you now know sand
where there once was river in your inner parts;

when you are ready
to say – I have done terrible things,
and there is a room somewhere that holds
this evidence, a thumbprint
made in blood;

then this creed is for you.
We belong to a single country,
and this is our sad anthem.

A Smaller Song

for Thomas Glave

Jamaica 2006

Thomas, a boy has died. I did not know him. I did not mourn him. This isn't his elegy. I found him by mistake, his body tucked neatly into the corner of a newspaper. I had been looking for something else, and there he was, this murdered boy, and the article that accounted for his life seemed to me such a small thing, a whole world suggested in the margins and between the lines, this article that said but refused to say so many things. I did not know the boy, but neither did his killers.

The article said he was a softer boy than most. Long eyelashes. And he wanted to go to art school. He had moved in with his big brother and this is what made the neighbours frown. They said, 'Two man cannot live in the same house. It is against the laws of morality. Don't you know that we kill battybwoy here?' And so they killed him.

He had gone outside one night because, I imagine, the house was small, and he was thinking of his future which would not fit into the living room of that house. Portmore houses can be stifling. He went outside to neighbours who were offended by his softness and his eyelashes and this unforgivable fact – that he lived with a brother who, like all brothers, was male. His big brother who loved him, and who would find him minutes later, his eyes fluttering, his lips trembling, and the night full of the sound of him gargling on his own blood. And I imagine that when the killers walked away, their guns pressed between their trousers and their hips, they were humming. And Thomas, I know you know this thing keeps on happening, that this tune of murderers is too often hummed, and though still many of us say such things don't happen, and we tuck these deaths away in the corners of newspapers.

Today a woman phones her son. Her mouth is sweet with gossip. She speaks of a man at the University of the West Indies who was not killed yesterday – who was saved although, she says, he did not deserve salvation. Although his life had been made forfeit. Although the mob of angry students who chased him from a toilet where he was doing something the newspapers cannot print, made rightful demands of his heart and his liver and all of his insides which were no longer his but theirs. Although the crowd reminded the guards into whose small room the man had run – that *nasty people like him must dead!* And on the phone this mother agrees to her son that nasty people must dead. And in this moment, a son knows that his mother does not love him. Her words, to him, are like black pepper buried at the crossroads with his name on it. The son imagines himself, his small body delivered to the crowd of students, and then slaughtered. He imagines his mother humming over his corpse, a tune whose notes have stretched over wars and crusades, the song of crows, its melody as crisp as burnt flesh, the tune hummed by killing neighbours.

And Thomas, you raise up a song in response. And your song is as big as Heaven. Your song is the one that should have been in the mother's mouth. A brave and a terrible song. A song that we sometimes groan more than we can sing. And I am writing all of this to say that you must always continue to sing your song, even on the days when I cannot sing it with you, because you sing for the boy who died, and for the men in this country who were unfortunately saved, and those who unfortunately weren't. And you sing a song for Brian. But Thomas, to sing your song means we have to mount the pulpit of dead bodies, gain leverage from the crucified, and some days I cannot bear to do it. I cannot bear to look on the flat faces of the dead. I know the fight we must fight. My neighbours are humming each night. But please forgive me if there are days when I choose to sing a smaller song, because sometimes your song is bigger than my mouth.

I think of him often – Brian – his house which smelled of limes, the stone path that led to the perfect shade of his verandah. How he would tell us about the revolution being planned. But when your song rose over his body, your same song, as big as Heaven, full of mourning, full of what was lost – I suddenly felt I could not then sing for all he had given us. It was as if your voice which is always breaking the terrible silences had suddenly imposed another. So we had to pretend we were eternally defeated people. We had to pretend we were not Maroons after all. We had to send out letters to Amnesty as if we were shackled people begging Queen Victoria to set us free. We had to pretend no battles had been won when some had, and maybe they were not the big battles, maybe no treaty had been signed, but we had won small things. And Thomas, on days when the terribleness is too big, and your song is too big for my mouth, and the sadness of this island comes upon me like wings, and I think I want to fly away from here, then I try to remember smaller things. I try to sing a smaller song.

I sing a smaller song for the magical ways we live underground. You might say that is not to live; it is the same as death and coffins. You might say *only days above ground are good days*. But I believe there is a great spirit under the earth, and there is a power in this way that we keep company with the dead, learning how to float as poltergeists, soucouyant, old hig, bodiless beings that could possess you if you were found walking one night without a crucifix. And some days I choose to sing for that.

I sing a smaller song because we gather. Because as awful as this island can be, I have known men from the Antilles who have come here because their own islands were too lonely. I sing for those far houses in Stony Hill, and Jacks Hill, and the verandah of Brian's house where we have met under the cover of music and sweat. I sing because of the lyrics we have always been able turn on their heads. Boom bye bye to who? We are still here. Thomas, I sing because we gather, and because we dance.

I sing a smaller song for the way we know to talk our talk. The way we speak loudly but only the right people can hear us. I sing for this secret – our creole, lyrical and coded as drums. And this smaller song that I sing, some days I sing it in that language.

I sing a smaller song for the ways we exist flamboyantly and invisibly at the same time. The ways we exist incredibly. Haven't you seen us in New Kingston? In gold shirts. In pocketless pants. Haven't you seen the bold transgression of our hips? Haven't you heard the sirens of our lisps. And despite it all, we dodge the radars. We limbo away from bullets. We live our incredible and abundant lives. And isn't that something, Thomas? Some days, isn't it enough to sing about?

For the Pilots

Two RAF air crew died after their low-flying jet plunged into the Rest and Be Thankful hill face and exploded into flames. Scotland, 2 July 2009.

Rest and be thankful
    You knew the balance of wings
    You were familiar with clouds
    You blazed a way home.

A Short History of Beds We Have Slept in Together

Jamaica, 2002–2007

Every bed was made illegal by the brush
of chest against chest, and by our sweat.
We put pillows in our mouths and became full
of swallowed grunts and aaaahs.
We knew not to wake a universe with testimonies
as loud as our hair and the cut of our jeans,
those small ways of being which had pronounced
over us a sentence, but a sentence so short
it wasn't half of what we kept inside, chewing,
every night, on pillows.

Hull, Student Accommodation, October 2007

In the small bed that could not fit
our torsos side by side, we fell asleep
in opposite directions, and woke
hugging each other's legs, as if to hold them
from all directions that lead away.

Trinidad, July 2006

In Ashraph's room a bed would be too high:
we'd roll into his canvases and wake
with acrylic in our eyes, flecks of oil

on our thighs; we would unstill the colour
of Ashraph's room. A bed would be too high.
We lie on a pile of blankets; we make

love close to ground, and for a while
our eyes are as acrylic and our thighs

are as oil. And we become all the colour
of Ashraph's room. A bed would have been too high.

Apsley Street, Glasgow, 2008

I know you do not like
the way I write moments,
how they grow into some kind of magic
you do not always recognise.
I know you think things are simpler
and it is enough to simply say
how things are – like this bed,
its large spread, the colour of tulips;
I know you will say, isn't it magic enough
that we fall asleep in the tangle of fingers,
that we sometimes dream a single dream.

A Prayer at Squire Street, 2009

Bless this home that we have bought –
each corner, each window, the high
and slanting roof; bless the colour
of our rooms, and then bless the rooms
that shall know us better than we know ourselves.
Bless the stairs that our door opens to,
may we always ascend into our home
in peace.
This used to be a church, so blessings should come
easy. Now bless our bed, the first
we have bought together;
bless its board and its sponge.
May we never grow weary of love.

Epilogue

Let us not repeat the easy lies about eternity
and love. We have fallen out of love
before – like children surpassing
the borders of their beds, woken
by gravity, the suddenness of tiles.
So it is we have opened our eyes
in the dark, found ourselves far
from all that was safe and soft.
So it is we have nursed red bruises.
If we are amazed at anything let it be this:
not that we have fallen from love,
but that we were always resurrected
into it, like children who climb sweetly
back to bed.

The Law Concerning Mermaids

There was once a law concerning mermaids. My friend thinks it a
wondrous thing – that the British Empire was so thorough it had
invented a law for everything. And in this law it was decreed: were
any to be found in their usual spots, showing off like dolphins,
sunbathing on rocks – they would no longer belong to themselves.
And maybe this is the problem with empires: how they have forced
us to live in a world lacking in mermaids – mermaids who under-
stood that they simply were, and did not need permission to exist
or to be beautiful. The law concerning mermaids only caused
mermaids to pass a law concerning man: that they would never
again cross our boundaries of sand; never again lift their torsos up
from the surf; never again wave at sailors, salt dripping from their
curls; would never again enter our dry and stifling world.

What We Thought Were Signs

I love that doctors are not impressed
by our symptoms. We tell them,
this morning I shat blood; and I faint

three or four times a day; and always
after I have eaten salt. And they say,
This is nothing to worry about.

They rescue us from our nightly vigils,
the way we had become insomniacs
who kept detailed journals of the dark

movements in our bodies, who held
fast to the belief that if death comes
to the sleeping, we ought to stay awake.

I love that doctors refuse to blink
at what we thought were signs of our sure
and impending ends, these bright spots

of red in the toilet. But we still smile
because our doctors say
the simple things we need them to say:

take a deep breath now; don't worry;
you're going to be okay.

On the Ninth Night

The night, full of bread and salt. The hours flicker like candles.

The Singerman's mouth, round as the stone no longer

at the river. The lid lifted from the pot; the goat's head risen;

the teeth of the goat as white as the teeth of your dead mother.

The world, as empty as cupboards. Your tears, fallen into the pot;

your grief like a seasoning. The drum rolling like a stone to Babylon.

The night full of bread and salt; the hours flickering like candles.

The Singerman's Other Job

In late hours the Singerman can be found
at a dead yard, pointing songs to the moon
if there is a moon, to the dark if there is only dark.
For this, the Singerman is paid with rum.
If it takes all night he will sing all night, until
his melody is as sure as what he builds in the daytime.
The dead will step on roofs, on trees; they will float
up to the stars, towards an intergalactic highway
where comets and angels pass. There is a road
that climbs towards Mount Zion, and this too
was built by the Singerman.

A Parting Song

May your portion be blue
     May your portion be sky
May your portion be light,
     Goodbye.

And may your portion be song
     Whose notes never die
And may the music be sweet,
     Goodbye.

And may your portion be soft
     And may your portion be love
Yes, may your portion be love
     And may your portion be soft
And may the soft lift you high
     And may your portion be sky
Goodbye.

A Nine Night Song

When you cross River Jurdan
Tell Liza how-di-do
Tell her, listen to wi song
Cause we singing it fi you
Tell her wi love and wi missing
Stretch more than every mile
But we patient in de trodding
And we see her in a while

When you cross River Jurdan
Tell mi mumma how-di-do
Tell her, listen to wi song
Cause we singing it fi you
Tell her wi love and wi missing
Is a fruit that cannot spwile
But we patient in de trodding
And we see her in a while

Noctiphobia

for my grandmother

Because she was wife to the tall preacherman, Pentecostongued,
whose every word whipped fire, whose oiled thumb

pressed on women's foreheads made them wheel and turn
then turn again like dogs under the spell of their own tails

and because she wore the gold ring he bought
with Yankee dollars earned from digging through Panama

and they lay on a cot in a cool red house with bamboo
doors, never locked, a devilman stole in

one night, women's jealous money in pocket,
cemetery dirt in hands which he rubbed

onto her belly; each time my grandmother swelled
with child an iron tide rose and drowned the baby.

Six times she felt a sudden stillness at midnight,
learned how to vomit out the foetus

but my grandmother believed curse-breaking magic
lived in the number seven. The familiar

motion of a being inside sent her marching up
to riverhead to sprinkle her belly with water.

The child was christened with seven names
all meaning, 'de lion who bruk up de chains'

and he is a tall preacherman, Pentecostongued
whose every word whips fire. The devilman is dead,

choked on fishbone when he saw my grandmother approach,
baby sucking from her tit. But I only remember her dying

shivering on a cot, singing, *Why should I fear de night or de pestilence which walketh inside it?*

Some Definitions for Night

— the time which follows evening like the next carriage of a train.
A justification for candles and by extension love whose
pronouncement is made easier in dark spaces, over small
flickering flames and a cascade of wax.   Night is a storing
place for creatures that have not been named yet; a mammalogist
says of a purple, rhombus-shaped creature – *it's as if it just
stepped out of night where it had been hiding.*   Night is a habitat
for dreams, the acre of forest inside us.   Night cannot be
measured by the second or the hour hand. It is its own time,
requiring only that we breathe deeply.   Night is a large womb,
a spectacularly bloated pregnancy. Entire planets are born from
night.   And night is an opening chapter I am yet to write; it
will include peeniwallies, the terrible red-eyed Rolling Calf,
and the following instruction: turn these pages slowly – push
the sun down, down, below the horizon – and a story will
come to steal your breath.